Mel Bay Presents

Illustrated Method for

Flute

Sheridon W. Stokes & Richard A. Condon

Fifth Edition

*I am eternally grateful to the late Richard Condon (my friend and co-author)
for the inspiration and hard work he did in helping me prepare this book.*

Art Director .... Robert A. Shepard
Cover/Graphic Design and Illustration .... Joseph P. Lanning
Photography .... Martin Novell, M.F.T.
Production Support .... Teresa L. Vang

Sheridon Stokes Music (BMI)
2461 Santa Monica Blvd., Suite 133
Santa Monica, CA 90404
On the web: www.flute-music.com
email: ssmpublish@aol.com

Visit us on the Web at www.melbay.com — E-mail us at email@melbay.com

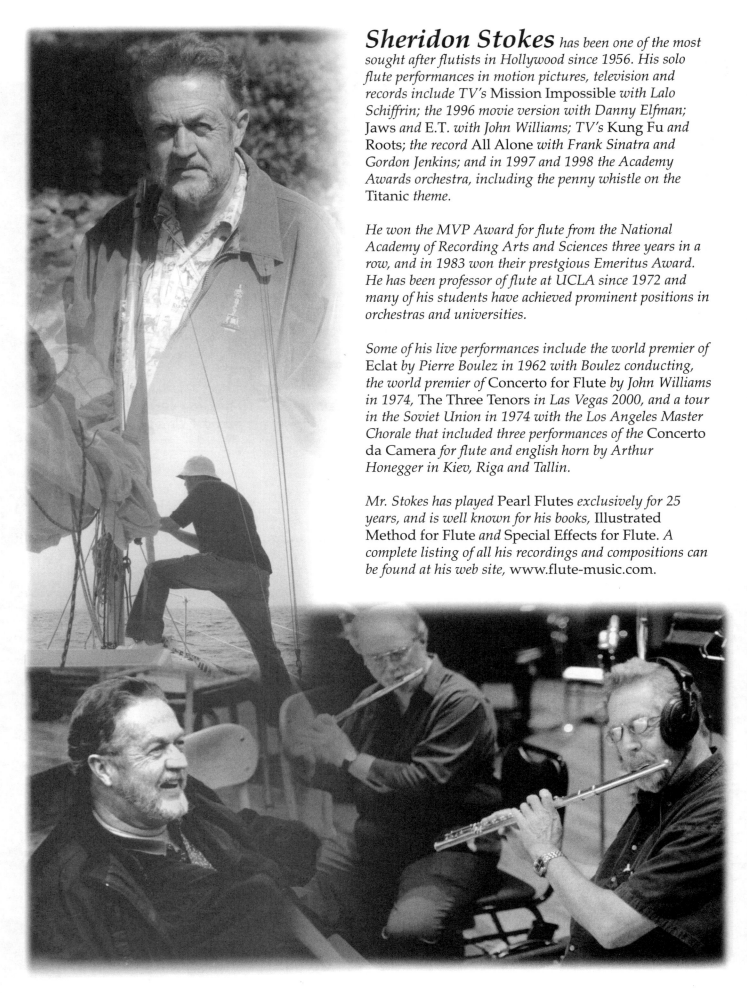

Sheridon Stokes *has been one of the most sought after flutists in Hollywood since 1956. His solo flute performances in motion pictures, television and records include TV's* Mission Impossible *with Lalo Schiffrin; the 1996 movie version with Danny Elfman;* Jaws *and* E.T. *with John Williams; TV's* Kung Fu *and* Roots; *the record* All Alone *with Frank Sinatra and Gordon Jenkins; and in 1997 and 1998 the Academy Awards orchestra, including the penny whistle on the* Titanic *theme.*

He won the MVP Award for flute from the National Academy of Recording Arts and Sciences three years in a row, and in 1983 won their prestgious Emeritus Award. He has been professor of flute at UCLA since 1972 and many of his students have achieved prominent positions in orchestras and universities.

Some of his live performances include the world premier of Eclat *by Pierre Boulez in 1962 with Boulez conducting, the world premier of* Concerto for Flute *by John Williams in 1974,* The Three Tenors *in Las Vegas 2000, and a tour in the Soviet Union in 1974 with the Los Angeles Master Chorale that included three performances of the* Concerto da Camera *for flute and english horn by Arthur Honegger in Kiev, Riga and Tallin.*

Mr. Stokes has played Pearl Flutes *exclusively for 25 years, and is well known for his books,* Illustrated Method for Flute *and* Special Effects for Flute. *A complete listing of all his recordings and compositions can be found at his web site,* www.flute-music.com.

Foreword

This is the first book I have seen which presents in some depth the fundamentals of flute technique through discussion, illustration and photography. It is refreshing to encounter such a book in a field in which a collection of exercises is frequently presented under the guise of a "method" and no discussion of how to play the flute given. I think the authors have done an excellent job, and taken a major step forward in musical instruction.

- Jean-Pierre Rampal

Preface

Unlike many flute books which give long series of exercises, but no instruction on how to play the flute, the *Illustrated Method for Flute* uses the resources of language, illustration, and photography to help you to learn to play the flute quickly and successfully. The *Illustrated Method for Flute* is a book of instructions based not only on the musical and teaching experience of its authors, but also on current research in the physics of sound production in the flute and physiological and anatomical aspects of flute playing. The authors would like to thank the many people whose advice and assistance have been of inestimable help in shaping the text, viz., the late Haakon Bergh, Arthur Gleghorn, Louella Howard, William Green, Mitchell Lurie, Woodson Baldwin, James Gear, Eileen Anderson, Drs. Koike and Yanagihara of the University of Southern California Institute of Laryngology, and Karen Ailor, who edited the manuscript for publication. Production of the fifth edition was the work of Robert Shepard, Joseph Lanning, Martin Novell and Teresa Vang. Models for the photographs were Jennifer Dean, Jared Ferguson, Gary Foster, Sean Greener, Hami Jin, Aisha Marshall, Amy Phillips, Catherine Schult, Fred Selden and Michael Stokes.

Contents

Figure 1.

Figure 2.

Assembling the Flute

Assembling the Flute

The flute consists of three sections – a head joint, a body tube, and a foot joint. In joining the three together (Figures 1 and 2), the student must properly align the sections while avoiding possible damage to the key rod mechanisms. *When assembling the flute never hold the sections by the key rods, as they can be damaged very easily.* Instead, hold them by the areas where there are no keys (e.g., the bottom of the foot joint and the top of the body tube). When the three are assembled, rotate the head joint until the center of the embouchure hole is in line with the center of the majority of keys in the body tube. Now turn the foot joint so that the rod to which its keys are attached is in line with the center line of the majority of keys on the body tube (see Figure 3). If you hold the foot joint to your eye and look down the flute (Figure 4), the center of the embouchure hole, the center of the keys on the body tube, and the rod on the foot joint should all be approximately in alignment. *When you rotate the sections to align them, do not put any pressure on the key rods.*

Figure 3.

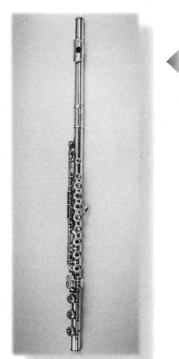

Figure 4.

1

Assembling the Flute

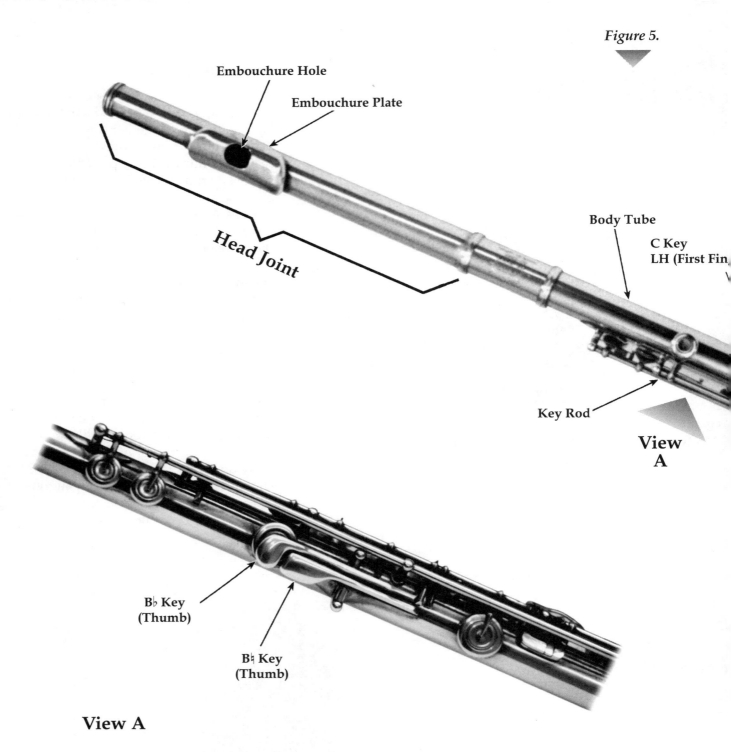

Figure 5.

Embouchure Hole

Embouchure Plate

Body Tube

C Key
LH (First Fin...

Head Joint

Key Rod

View
A

B♭ Key
(Thumb)

B♮ Key
(Thumb)

View A

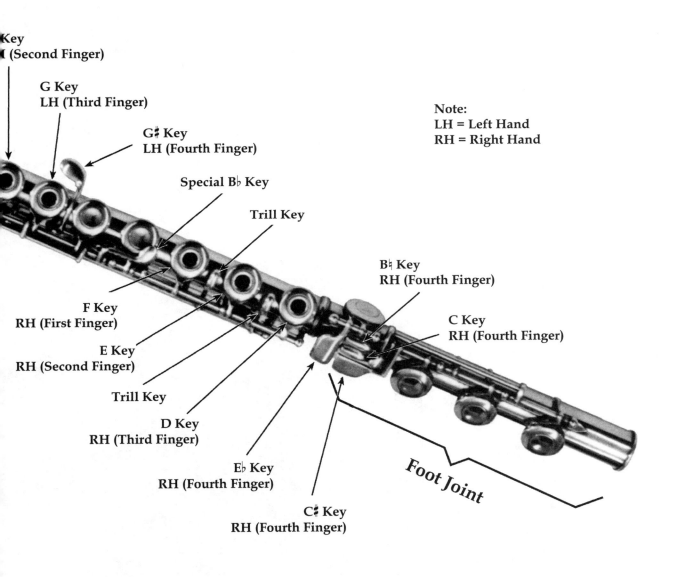

Key
(Second Finger)

G Key
LH (Third Finger)

G♯ Key
LH (Fourth Finger)

Special B♭ Key

Trill Key

F Key
RH (First Finger)

E Key
RH (Second Finger)

Trill Key

D Key
RH (Third Finger)

E♭ Key
RH (Fourth Finger)

C♯ Key
RH (Fourth Finger)

Note:
LH = Left Hand
RH = Right Hand

B♮ Key
RH (Fourth Finger)

C Key
RH (Fourth Finger)

Foot Joint

Balancing the Flute

Balancing the Flute

An important consideration in playing the flute is to achieve maximum freedom for the fingers so that they can execute their proper role – i.e., depressing and releasing the various keys. Any finger used to support the flute is not completely free to finger notes. The trick, therefore, is to support the flute while involving the fingers as little as possible.

Always remember that *the flute is balanced, not held.* To understand what this means, take the assembled flute and rest the head joint against your lower lip. Place the first finger of the left hand on the body tube of the flute in the manner shown in Figure 6, and with the palm of the right hand push the foot joint of the flute away from you. You will find that the flute remains in place even though your fingers are not "holding

Index Finger of left hand Serves as Fulcrum

Right Hand Thrusts Forward

Figure 6. ▶

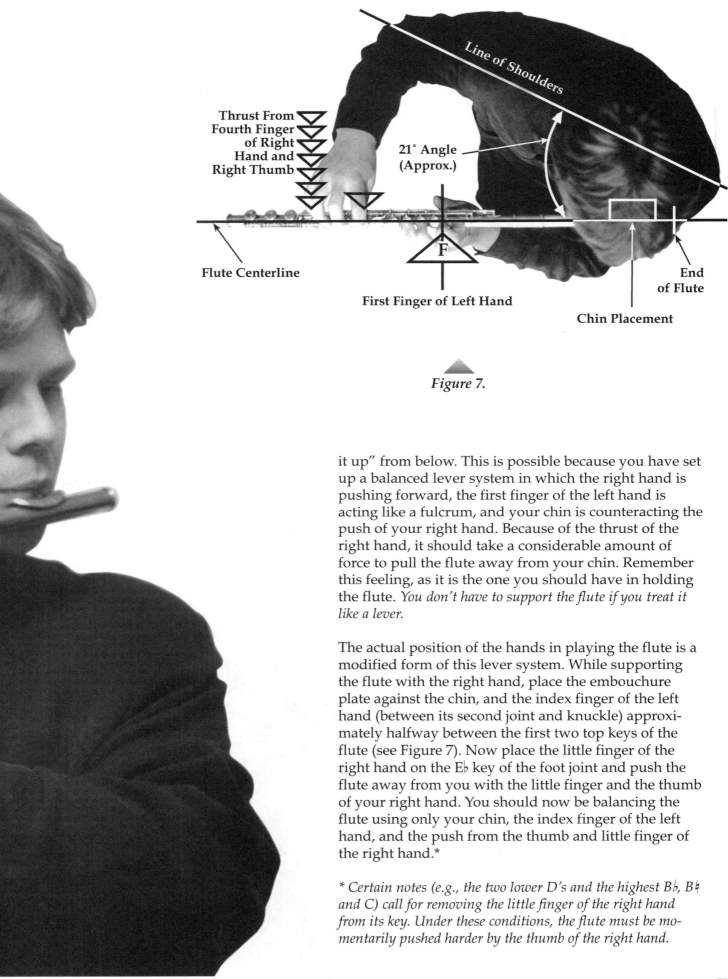

Figure 7.

it up" from below. This is possible because you have set up a balanced lever system in which the right hand is pushing forward, the first finger of the left hand is acting like a fulcrum, and your chin is counteracting the push of your right hand. Because of the thrust of the right hand, it should take a considerable amount of force to pull the flute away from your chin. Remember this feeling, as it is the one you should have in holding the flute. *You don't have to support the flute if you treat it like a lever.*

The actual position of the hands in playing the flute is a modified form of this lever system. While supporting the flute with the right hand, place the embouchure plate against the chin, and the index finger of the left hand (between its second joint and knuckle) approximately halfway between the first two top keys of the flute (see Figure 7). Now place the little finger of the right hand on the E♭ key of the foot joint and push the flute away from you with the little finger and the thumb of your right hand. You should now be balancing the flute using only your chin, the index finger of the left hand, and the push from the thumb and little finger of the right hand.*

* Certain notes (e.g., the two lower D's and the highest B♭, B♮ and C) call for removing the little finger of the right hand from its key. Under these conditions, the flute must be momentarily pushed harder by the thumb of the right hand.

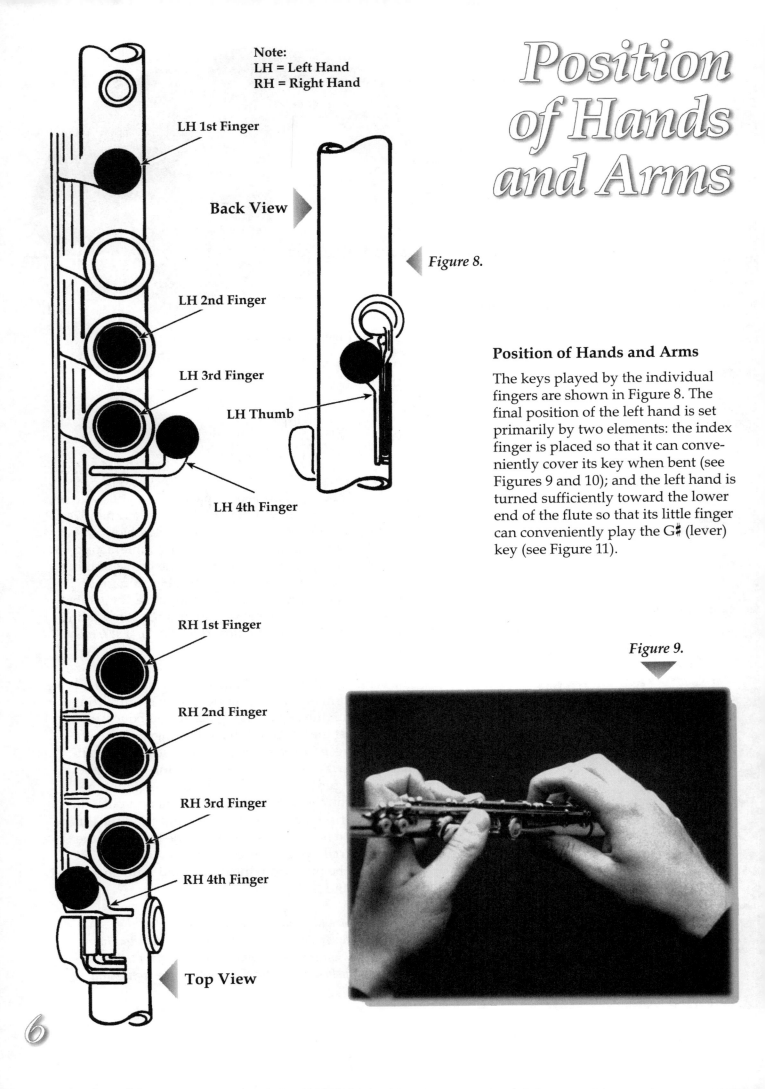

Note:
LH = Left Hand
RH = Right Hand

LH 1st Finger

Back View

Figure 8.

LH 2nd Finger

LH 3rd Finger

LH Thumb

LH 4th Finger

RH 1st Finger

RH 2nd Finger

RH 3rd Finger

RH 4th Finger

Top View

Position of Hands and Arms

Position of Hands and Arms

The keys played by the individual fingers are shown in Figure 8. The final position of the left hand is set primarily by two elements: the index finger is placed so that it can conveniently cover its key when bent (see Figures 9 and 10); and the left hand is turned sufficiently toward the lower end of the flute so that its little finger can conveniently play the G# (lever) key (see Figure 11).

Figure 9.

The position of the right hand is set by the right thumb, which should be placed in a bent position (see Figure 12) under the flute about halfway between the index and second fingers of that hand. The right hand is held in such a way (Figure 13) that you do not have to shift your wrist or arm toward the foot of the flute to play the lowest keys (C♯, C, and B♮ if available).

Figure 10.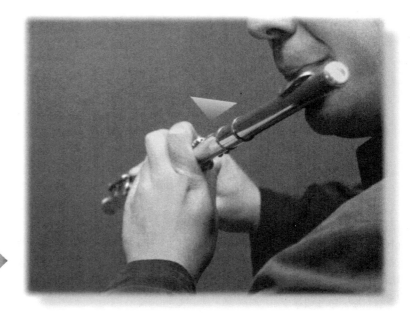

Figure 11.

Figure 12.

Position of Hands and Arms

For complete freedom of finger motion, the fingers should be slightly arched (this has the effect of raising the palms slightly), and the wrists held as shown (see Figure 14). A word of caution is in order: beginners are often tempted to support the flute with the left hand (especially with the thumb). *This should never be done,* as it hinders the motion of the fingers of the left hand and immobilizes the thumb. If you find yourself doing this when you play, go back to the lever arrangement described above, removing both thumbs from the underside of the flute. This will remind you of the feeling you should have in balancing the flute.

Figure 13.

Figure 14.

Figure 15.

Posture

Incorrect Posture

Posture

Proper posture is important not only to fingering (it is almost impossible to play fast passages with faulty arm position), but also to breathing and breath control, a central concern with any wind instrument. If you are slumped forward or down (Figures 15 and 16), you will not be able to take in enough air or to control its expenditure in playing. Since flute playing depends essentially on the delivery of an ample, unimpeded column of air to your lips, you cannot play effectively in a posture which makes inhaling and exhaling difficult.

Figure 16.

Incorrect Posture

Figures 15 & 16. Incorrect posture. The player must lift the entire upper part of the body with each inhalation. Bending the neck forward cuts off both the intake and expulsion of air. Bad posture frequently results in a thin, feeble tone and faulty breath control.

Posture

Proper posture (see Figures 17 and 18) requires keeping the elbows away from the body (usually about six inches) and the torso and head erect, not slumped forward. The left shoulder is thrust forward about 21° and the right shoulder rotated backwards. The flute is held approximately parallel to the floor.

Correct Posture

▲

Figure 18.

Figure 17.

▼

Correct Posture

Figures 17 & 18. Correct posture. Keeping your torso and head erect makes it possible to breathe with a minimum of effort and deliver an unrestricted column of air to the flute. Arms are far enough away from the body not to interfere with breathing.

Figures 19 & 20. Normal breathing is quite shallow; we take in only a few cups of air at a time. To play a wind instrument such as the flute, we must learn how to take in and control the use of large amounts of breath.

Breathing and Breath Control

A great deal of attention is rightfully paid to the placement and shaping of the lips (embouchure) in playing the flute. What is often overlooked, however, is that *the flute is a wind instrument. Its performance is critically dependent on the amount of air the player is delivering and the way in which it is delivered.* Embouchure is merely a final modification of this air supply. *Poor air column control* (tightening the throat, not using abdominal muscles properly, having insufficient or too much air for the tongue to release, etc.) *is a basic cause of many difficulties in playing the flute.* Students can waste much time in experimenting with embouchure changes when the cause of their problem lies in the improper use of lungs and abdomen. Because the fundamentals of good flute playing lie in these organs, as well as in the lips, we shall give a rather extensive account of the principles of breathing. *Time spent in reading and applying these principles will contribute substantially to* the student's progress on the flute. We will consider breathing in two parts – inhaling and exhaling.

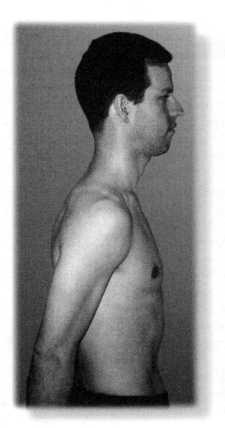

Figure 19.

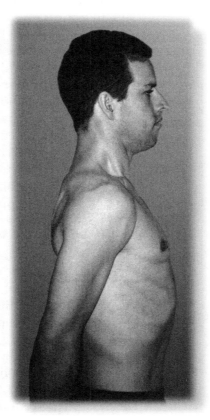

Figure 20.

Inhaling - Ordinarily we breathe very shallowly, taking in only a small fraction of our lung capacity (Figure 19). Shallow breathing is perfectly suited to our ordinary activities, but it is completely inadequate for playing the flute. To play the flute, we have to learn how to inhale very large amounts of air (Figure 20). This can be done readily once you understand how your body works.

When your body is getting an insufficient supply of oxygen, you feel tired. One symptom of being tired is yawning, which is nature's way of getting more oxygen into the body. When you yawn, your throat relaxes and opens up to a maximum extent, and your sides push outward, thus expanding the lung cavity. This is how nature gets oxygen to us when we need it. Breathing in when playing the flute is merely a modification and extension of this process.

Breathing and Breath Control

Although we have the feeling that we are drawing air into our lungs when we breathe, in fact all we are doing is expanding our chest cavity. Atmospheric pressure is pressing down on all parts of our body at about 15 pounds per square inch. When we expand our chest cavity, there is suddenly less air pressure in our lungs than there is in the surrounding atmosphere. As a result, air rushes in to equalize the pressure. We call this activity inhalation. The key to inhaling is expanding the chest cavity.

Figure 21 shows the two primary means nature has provided for expanding the chest cavity. First, there is the diaphragm, a dome-shaped muscle that extends horizontally across the body near the lower ribs. Below the diaphragm are the stomach, intestines, and other abdominal organs. When we contract the diaphragm it flattens out, pushing down and compressing the abdominal organs. As the diaphragm pushes the abdominal organs down, it enlarges the chest cavity, which is subsequently filled up with air.

To feel the diaphragm at work, sit on the end of a chair with your elbows on your knees in the attitude of *The Thinker*, and take a deep breath. You will feel the diaphragm compressing the abdominal organs, and the lungs moving down to occupy the newly available space.

The second way in which we expand the chest cavity is by pushing our ribs outward. As Figure 21 shows, our ribs form a drooping cage which is attached to breast and back bones by flexible cartilage. Between the ribs lie the intercostal muscles. When we breath, these and other muscles pull the ribs upward and outward. The flexible cartilage gives slightly to permit this motion. The chest cavity is thus enlarged and air automatically rushes into it. Because the lowest (floating) ribs are not attached to the bone and the lower ribs have longer cartilage attachments, the lower portion of the rib cage is more flexible than the upper. Thus we tend to feel maximum expansion taking place in the lower, rather than upper, portion of the rib cage.

Figure 21.

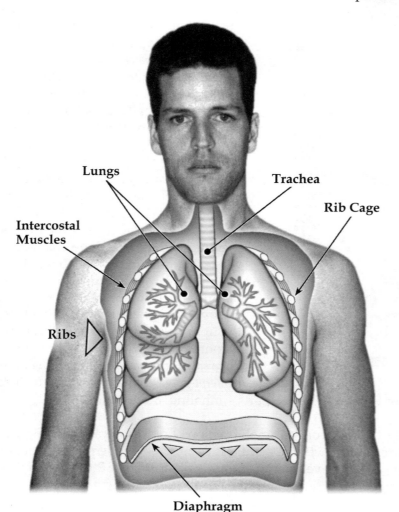

Lungs

Trachea

Rib Cage

Intercostal Muscles

Ribs

Diaphragm

Figure 21. *In inhaling, the diapraghm pushes down on the abdominal organs, enlarging the cavity which contains the lungs, and filling the lungs with air.*

Figure 22.

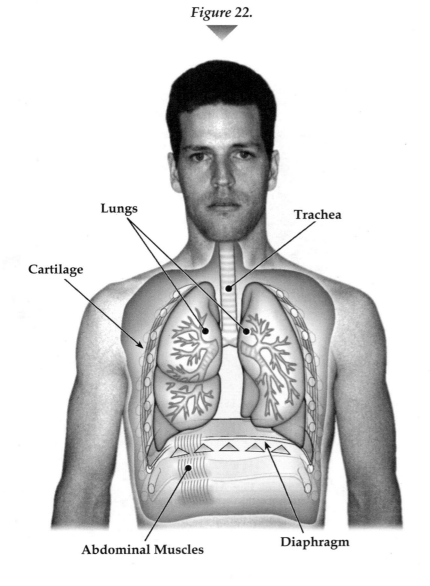

Lungs

Trachea

Cartilage

Abdominal Muscles

Diaphragm

Figure 22. In exhaling, the muscles of the abdomen and sides pull in, forcing the abdominal organs and diaphragm upward like a piston, and expelling the air from the lungs.

When asked to take a deep breath, beginning students often crane their necks, raise their shoulders, and pull in their stomachs. *Precisely the opposite set of motions is required for good breathing.* The throat opens as widely as possible (as in a yawn), the shoulders remain in place, and the stomach is pushed out as the air is inhaled.

As we remarked earlier, proper breathing and proper posture are inseparably connected. If you are slumped forward, for example, you have to raise the entire weight of the upper body in order to take a breath. Similarly, if you have your head tilted down toward your chest, you constrict your throat, thus inhibiting both inhalation and exhalation. Good breathing and good posture are much like the two members of an optical illusion: without one, the other does not appear.

Exhaling - Inhaling only assures that you will have enough air to play the flute. Of the two actions involved in the breathing cycle, exhaling is the more difficult, for it involves the controlled delivery of this air supply to the lips. When we breathe out normally, we do so without apparent effort or any awareness of muscular action. When we exhale air with consistent pressure behind it – such as blowing up a balloon – we sense that exhaling can bring several sets of muscles into play, primarily those on the sides of the chest cavity and the abdominal and waist muscles. *The act of exhaling into the flute is much like blowing up a balloon.* It involves deliberately sustaining the pressure of an air column by consciously exercising certain muscles.

Two sets of muscles – those of the sides of the chest cavity, and those of the abdomen and waist – are used in controlling the expulsion of air (see Figure 22). The chest cavity can be likened to a bellows. When the sides of the cavity are pulled in, air is expelled (see Figures 23 and 24). Aiding these muscles are those of the abdomen and waist which pull in, forcing the already compressed abdominal organs upward, and pushing the diaphragm upward to its original domed position. As a result of this action, the chest cavity is reduced, and air is expelled.

Breathing and Breath Control

Figure 23. *To experience the firmness your stomach muscles should have, try playing the flute while seated with your feet held parallel to the floor.*

Figure 23. ▶

Figures 24 & 25. *The whole breathing mechanism can be likened to a bellows. When the diaphragm (which corresponds to accordion-pleated leather) pushes down, the bellows (lungs) fill up with air. When the muscles of the sides and stomach (the handles of the bellows) are pushed in, air is forced out of the system.*

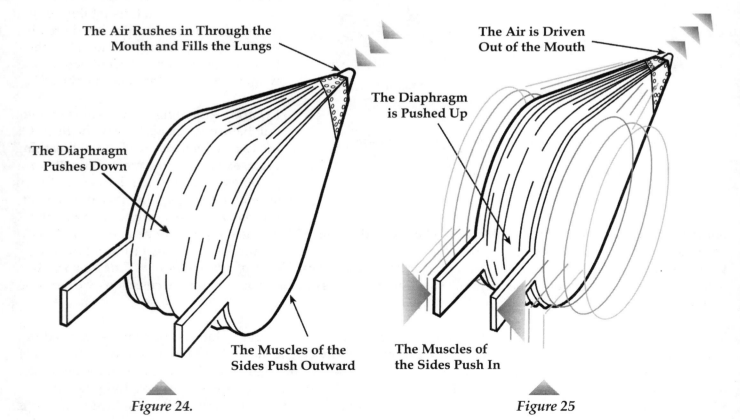

The Air Rushes in Through the
Mouth and Fills the Lungs

The Air is Driven
Out of the Mouth

The Diaphragm
is Pushed Up

The Diaphragm
Pushes Down

The Muscles of the
Sides Push Outward

The Muscles of
the Sides Push In

Figure 24.

Figure 25

Figure 24. *Inhalation is like filling a bellows with air.*

Figure 25. *Exhalation is like forcing air out of a bellows.*

In ordinary breathing, we let the diaphragm relax back into its original position in an uncontrolled manner. When we play the flute, we push the diaphragm back in a controlled and deliberate way by contracting the muscles of the stomach and sides. The diaphragm pushes down, as though one were lifting a weight, and the muscles of the stomach and sides pull in, thus forcing the diaphragm up under pressure. The result is a feeling of abdominal firmness which results from the dynamic tension of these two opposing forces. When a flutist plays loudly, the abdomen and side muscles pull in forcefully while the diaphragm remains relatively relaxed. As a result, the diaphragm moves upward quickly, expelling large amounts of air. When a flutist plays softly, the abdomen and side muscles pull in forcefully but the diaphragm is kept tense. This results in a dynamic tension between the two sets of muscles, so that the diaphragm moves upward slowly and smaller amounts of air are expelled *in a controlled manner.* The control comes from the dynamic tension between the two sets of opposing muscles.

The situation may be thought of as a tug of war. When the diaphragm is pushed back up quickly, much air is expelled quickly so that the notes are played *forte.* When the diaphragm gives up slowly, the air is expelled more slowly so that the notes are played *piano.* This leads to an unexpected turn of events: it takes more abdominal tension to play softly than it does to play loudly. In fact the softer you play, the more abdominal stress you should experience.

When asked to play loud or high, the tendency of beginning students is to tighten up their throats. The effect of this action is to cut off the air supply at the precise moment that it is needed. *To play loud or high, one pulls in the stomach, keeping the throat as open as possible.* The tone will be full, because the supply of air is plentiful and under pressure. The secret of a good flute tone lies as much in the stomach as it does in the embouchure of the player. William Kincaid used to call the diaphragm "the flutist's bow," and said that much of the technique of playing and phrasing is dependent upon the thorough development of the musculature surrounding the diaphragm.

"To play loud or high, one pulls in the stomach, keeping the throat as open as possible."

Exercises for Breath Control

Figure 26. Leg lifts: lie on back, raise feet 6″ off the floor; open and close legs.

Figure 26.

Figure 27.

Figure 27. William Kincaid attributed his remarkable breath control to the extensive swimming he did as a boy in Hawaii.

Figure 28.

Figure 29.

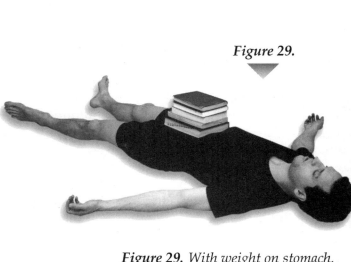

Figure 29. With weight on stomach, breathe deeply, lifting weight with stomach; release breath slowly.

Figure 28. Running helps to develop diaphragmatic breathing.

Figure 30. Leg lifts: lie on back and raise legs alternately off the floor.

Figure 30.

Exercises For Breath Control

Lung capacity and breath control can be developed in several ways other than by practicing on the flute. Swimming, for example, is an excellent conditioner for the breathing system, as is running or mountain climbing. Such exercises have been popular with several eminent flutists. Abdominal strengthening exercises are effective in firming up the muscles of the waist and abdomen, which play such an important role in forcing the air out of the lungs. In general, any exercise which causes you to breathe deeply (e.g., running), or which develops those muscles used to expel air (e.g., leg lifts), should contribute substantially to your performance. Practiced regularly, the exercises on these pages will improve your breath control (and hence tone and phrasing) on the flute.

Figure 31.

Figure 32. Leg raises: raise both feet as shown, straighten legs, and lower slowly to floor.

Figure 31. Stretching: expel air, bend over and touch the floor. While inhaling, gradually return to erect position with arms extended. Hold breath, then exhale forcefully, touch toes, and repeat.

Figure 32.

Figure 33.

Figure 33. Abdominal crunches: with feet held firmly on floor, go from reclining to a semi-upright position.

Embouchure

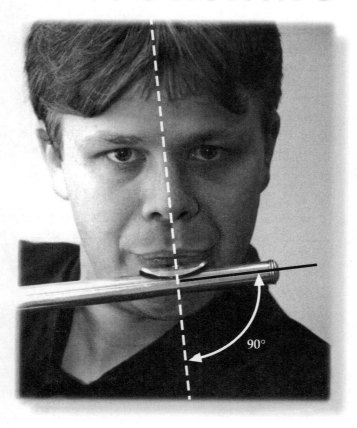

Embouchure

The term *embouchure* is used to describe the shaping and placing of the mouth in playing a wind instrument. The size and shape of the lip opening through which the breath exits, the relative tension of the lips, and location of the lips on the instrument – these and related aspects of the mouth formation and placement constitute the embouchure of a player.

Because it has a major effect upon the character of the musical tone produced, embouchure is one of the most important aspects of playing. Proper embouchure for the flute, while it is affected by the character of the individual player's mouth (e.g., the relative thickness of upper and lower lips, the jaw structure, etc.), is nevertheless determined fundamentally by the manner in which the flute produces sound.

Experiments with air systems such as the flute* have shown that the quality and character of the tone produced depend primarily upon three things: (1) the *speed* of the air jet; (2) the *distance* from the orifice (lip opening) to the edge; and (3) the *angle* at which the air jet strikes the edge. *Establishing the foundations of a good flute embouchure thus amounts to appropriately controlling these three things.*

Figure 34.

Those interested in pursuing the technical aspects of sound production in the flute should see the following works:

*Arthur Benade, **Horns, Strings, and Harmony,** (Doubleday and Company, Inc., Garden City, New York, 1960); Arthur Benade, **The Physics of Woodwinds,** Scientific American, October 1960; Sir James Jeans, **Science and Music** (Cambridge Press, Cambridge, England, 1937); W.L. Nyborg, M.D. Burkhard, and H.K. Schilling, **Acoustical Characteristics of Jet-Edge and Jet-Edge-Resonator Systems,** Journal of the Acoustical Society of America, Vol. 24, No. 3, May 1952, p. 293ff; N. Curle, **The Mechanics of Edge-Tones,** Proceedings of the Royal Society of London, Vol. 216, January-February 1953, p. 412ff.*

The work by Nyborg, Burkhard, and Schilling is especially thorough and examines the validity of Brown's empirical equation for jet-edge system, viz., f_e=0.466 ju/h, where f_e is the frequency of the edge-tone, u the linear air velocity, and h the distance from orifice to edge. The j term applies to the harmonic stage involved; thus j=1 for the fundamental, 2 for the first harmonic, etc. The equation is shown to be a good approximation for those frequencies within the compass of the flute. Our discussion above is based on the purport of this formula – namely, that the pitch produced on the flute (the edge-tone frequency amplified by a resonating cavity) is directly proportional to the linear air speed and inversely proportional to the orifice-to-edge distance. Dr. Nyborg has been kind enough to supply us with references to the following relevant dissertations: W.L. Nyborg, Ph.D. dissertation, Pennsylvania State University, 1947; M.D. Burkhard, M.S. thesis, Pennsylvania State University, 1950; C.L. Woodbridge, M.S. thesis, Pennsylvania State University, 1950; J. Bruce Brachenbridge, M.S. thesis, Brown University, 1957, and Ph.D. dissertation, Brown University, 1960.

*An excellent summary of the acoustics of the flute is given in John W. Coltman's article **The Acoustics of the Flute,** in Physics Today, November 1968 (Volume 21, No. 11), pgs. 25-32.*

Figures 34 & 35. In positioning the flute on the mouth, place the center line of the lips at the center of the embouchure hole. The flute should be parallel to the line formed by the junction of the lips. For middle register notes, most flutists cover about a quarter of the embouchure hole with their lower lips. (see Figure 35).

Figure 35. ▶

Figure 36. An edge tone is produced when a jet of air impinges on an edge, causing the formation of vortices or whirlpools. The pitch of the note produced increases as the velocity of the air jet increases, or as the orifice-to-edge distance decreases.

Whirlpools

Orifice

◀ *Figure 36.*

Edge

Air Jet

Figure 37. In the flute, the disturbances caused when the air jet impinges on the edge are communicated to the bore (shown in cross section) which functions like a sounding board. It picks up the sound of the edge tone and amplifies it, thus producing an audible musical tone.

Figure 37. ▶

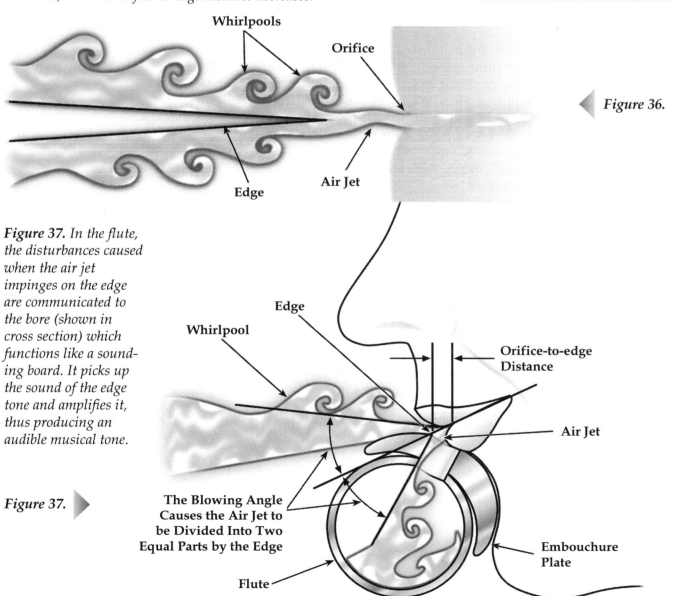

Edge

Whirlpool

Orifice-to-edge Distance

Air Jet

The Blowing Angle Causes the Air Jet to be Divided Into Two Equal Parts by the Edge

Embouchure Plate

Flute

19

Embouchure

The Three Major Elements of Flute Embouchure

1. The Speed of the Air Jet

The pitch produced depends in part upon the speed of the air jet. In general, high-speed jets produce high notes, and low-speed jets low notes. The speed of the air hitting the edge can be controlled either by the force with which one blows (harder or softer), the size of the opening between the lips, or both. For a given rate of blowing, the speed of the air jet increases as the size of the lip opening decreases. This can be demonstrated by blowing against the palm of your hand with an open mouth, and then gradually closing your mouth until only a small opening remains between the lips. The speed of the air striking your palm will increase during the process. In contrast, if you open your mouth, the speed of the air decreases.

2. Orifice-to-Edge Distance

The pitch produced can also be controlled by changing the distance between the orifice (lip opening) and the far edge of the blow hole. As you move your lips closer to the edge, the tone will go down in pitch slightly, then suddenly jump to a higher note (a harmonic of the first). Increasing the orifice-to-edge distance has the opposite effect. In general, high notes on the flute call for small lip-to-edge distances, while low notes require large lip-to-edge distances.

3. Angle of the Air Jet

Both tonal quality and amplitude (volume) are best when the edge divides the air jet into two equal parts. If you blow too much down into the flute or too high above the edge, the tone will decrease significantly in quality and amplitude. The proper angle for an individual mouth structure can be easily found by playing a sustained note and rotating the flute slightly. When the tone is loudest and brightest, the edge is splitting the air jet into two equal parts (i.e., you have established the proper blowing angle for that note). Because the lips move with respect to the edge, moving closer to it for high notes and farther from in for low notes, the blowing angle changes with pitch. For high notes, one must blow down on the edge (because the lips are close to it); for low notes, one blows more across at the edge (because the lips are farther from it). *The air jet, however, should always be split into two equal parts by the edge.*

These are the three basic factors of proper flute embouchure. In general, the following things take place as one plays from the lower through the upper registers:

Lower Register: Large opening between the lips; ample distance between lip opening and edge; air jet directed almost horizontally across the blow hole at the edge (see Figures 38 and 39).*

Middle Register: Opening between the lips decreases in size; lips move closer to edge; air jet is directed slightly down in order to be split by the edge (see Figures 40 and 41).

Upper Register: Very small opening between the lips; lips out over blow hole and brought close to the edge; air jet directed sharply down onto edge (see Figures 42 and 43).

Because the lower lip is pulled back from the edge as far as possible, it feels to some people as though they were blowing down into the flute for low notes.

Figures 38 & 39. The embouchure in the **lower register.**

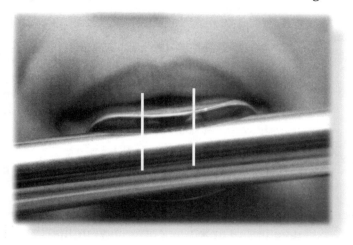

Figure 38.

Figure 39.

Figures 40 & 41. The embouchure in the **middle register.**

 Figure 40.

Figure 41.

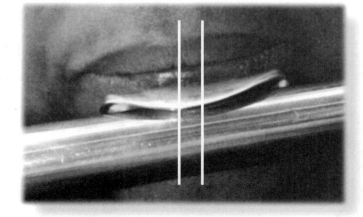

Figure 42.

Figures 42 & 43. The embouchure in the **upper register.**

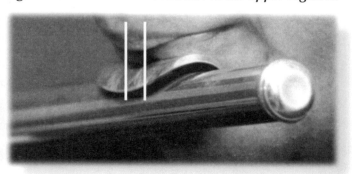

Figure 43.

21

Embouchure

Figure 44. *The interior of the mouth and throat have an important effect upon your tone. You should keep them both open as much as possible, as though you were on the verge of yawning. The jaw pushes down, forcing the mouth and throat open, and keeping the lips (which close to form the embouchure) in a state of dynamic tension.*

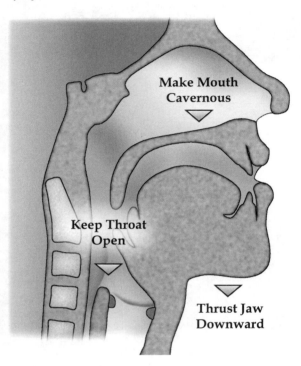

Make Mouth
Cavernous

Keep Throat
Open

Thrust Jaw
Downward

Figure 44.

It is very helpful to look into a mirror (see Figure 45) when you are developing your embouchure. Initially, you should hold the flute approximately parallel to the line formed by the juncture of your lips. Place the center of your lips in the center of the blow hole, covering about a quarter of the hole with your lower lip. Open your teeth until they are about one-fourth to one-half inch apart, and make the interior of your mouth as large as possible. Many people find that thinking of the beginning of a yawn helps them open up both the interior of their mouths and their throat passage. Now, keeping your upper lip firm, form an elliptical opening between your lips that looks like this ⬯. Do not make the ellipse too stretched like this ⬱ or purse the lips by collapsing the corners of the mouth. The corners should be firm, but not drawn up into a smile. Some flutists find it is helpful to think of saying the word "pure" in establishing the embouchure. You should always feel as though you are trying to form a circular opening, even though the result will in fact be a gentle ellipse ⬯. If you make the opening in your lips too round (pursing the lips), your tone will be fuzzy and hollow. Making the opening too lengthy, on the other hand, gives the tone a harsh, nasal quality. Your ear will help you reach an appropriate compromise.

Figure 45.

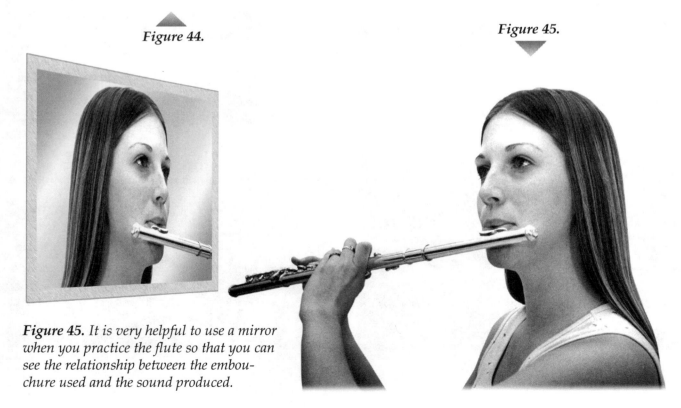

Figure 45. *It is very helpful to use a mirror when you practice the flute so that you can see the relationship between the embouchure used and the sound produced.*

The muscle which goes around the mouth (see Figure 46) is called the *orbicularis oris*. Radiating out from this muscle are more than twenty small muscles. Each of these can push or pull some portion of the *orbicularis oris* in some direction. For example, muscles which run up toward the nose in the center of the lips can depress it firmly against the upper teeth (depressors), or lift it away from the teeth into a buck-toothed smile (elevators). Muscularly, *flute embouchure is a dynamic balance of these many muscles.* You establish the proper elliptical shape for the opening and then induce a slight tension (not a hard tautness) into the muscles around the mouth to give the opening firmness and control. The jaw muscles lower the jaw in an effort to enlarge the opening. This is balanced by the upper lip which draws down over the teeth to close the opening. The corners of the mouth pull sideways to lengthen the opening; they are opposed by the muscles in the center of the lips which attempt to make the opening round. The result of all these opposing forces is a firm equilibrium of the lips.

Figure 46.

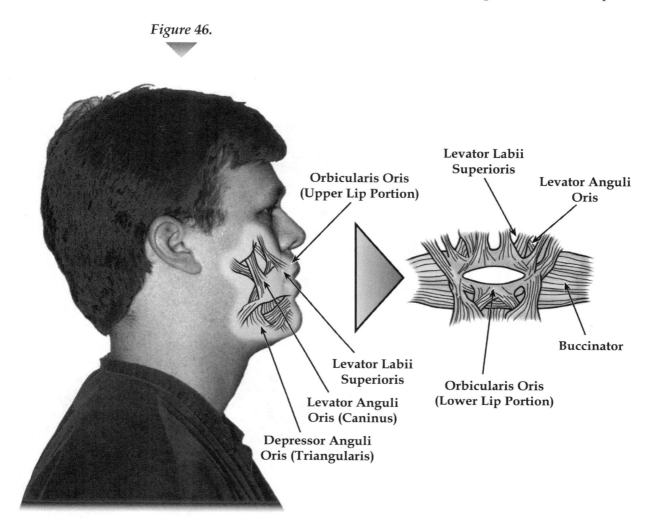

Orbicularis Oris
(Upper Lip Portion)

Levator Labii
Superioris

Levator Anguli
Oris

Levator Labii
Superioris

Levator Anguli
Oris (Caninus)

Depressor Anguli
Oris (Triangularis)

Orbicularis Oris
(Lower Lip Portion)

Buccinator

Figure 46. Muscularly, flute embouchure is like an even tug-of-war. The many muscles which surround the mouth pull against one another just enough to cancel each other's effect, thus inducing a firm (but not taut) muscular balance.

It has been suggested that forming the flute embouchure is much like grasping a straw between the lips, the difference being that the "straw" is a column of pressurized air whose shape and direction we can change at will.

As you play through the range of the flute, *the corners of your mouth should remain firm and relatively motionless.* Do not pout excessively for low notes, or draw the corners up into a tense smile for high notes. The motion of the lips toward and away from the edge and the changes in the size of the opening are made largely with the center portion of the lips, not by drawing in or retracting the corners of the mouth.

Embouchure

There are no known tricks that will enable you to develop a good flute embouchure overnight. What you can do, however, is to avoid some of the pitfalls which prevent progress on the flute by keeping in mind the following: the shape of the embouchure (a modified ellipse); the feel of the embouchure (firm but not tense); the three basic variables of embouchure (speed of air jet, distance from lip opening to edge, and angle of air jet). As you practice the flute, vary the last three factors until you achieve a pleasing, resonant tone. For example, turn the flute in and out and listen to the tone. When it is at its brightest, you have the optimum blowing angle. Now try moving closer to or farther away from the edge, or changing the size of the opening between your lips. Turn the flute in and out once again to establish the correct angle. If you experiment conscientiously in this manner and listen carefully to the sounds that result, you will be well on the way to establishing the appropriate embouchure for all portions of the flute's range.

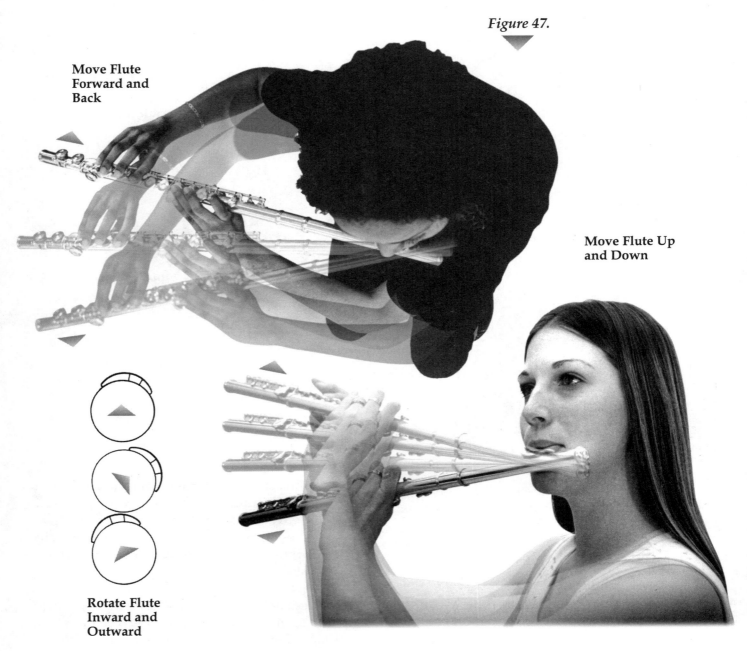

Figure 47.

Move Flute Forward and Back

Move Flute Up and Down

Rotate Flute Inward and Outward

Figure 47. *Practice should be regarded as a time for experimenting. Vary the placement of the flute and the embouchure, and observe the effects of these changes on tone quality and control.*

Dynamics, Range and Intonation

We remarked earlier that there is a close interplay between breath control and embouchure on the flute. Nowhere is this interplay more evident than in the areas of dynamics, range, and intonation. Dynamics refers to the relative loudness or softness with which a note is played. Intonation is the accuracy of pitch with which we play a note; either we play it in tune (good intonation), or we play it sharp or flat (poor intonation).

To appreciate the interplay between breath control and embouchure, take in a large supply of air, form a large O with your mouth, and expel the air rapidly (Figure 48). The main muscular actions you should feel are the muscles of the stomach and sides contracting. Now, take in another large supply of air, form a tiny pinhole opening with your mouth, and expel the air (Figure 49). This time the muscles of the stomach and sides do not contract rapidly, but they do become very tense and the diaphragm pushes down as though you were lifting a heavy weight. *These two conditions of the breath control muscles – a rapid pulling in of the muscles of the stomach and sides, and a state of dynamic tension of the abdominal muscles – are the two extremes of muscular control you should experience in playing the flute in tune throughout its dynamic range.* It is a good idea to practice these two extremes without a flute, just so that you will be familiar with them and remember how they feel.

Figure 48. Playing the flute loudly is like blowing up a large balloon. The muscles of the sides rapidly contract the chest cavity, and the air exits in large volumes from the large embouchure opening under little pressure.

◀ *Figure 48.*

Figure 49. ▶

Figure 49. Playing the flute softly is like blowing up a small balloon. The muscles of the sides and diaphragm are in a state of dynamic tension, and the air exits in small quantities from the small embouchure opening under great pressure.

Dynamics, Range and Intonation

The above experiment is intended to show you that playing loud on the flute requires a large embouchure opening amply supplied with air by an energetic *contraction* of the muscles of the stomach and sides. Playing softly on the flute requires a small embouchure opening accompanied by an energetic *tension* of the muscles of the stomach and sides. A good way to imagine this latter muscular set is to take in a supply of air and then pretend that someone is about to hit you in the stomach. It takes this kind of abdominal muscular stress to play high notes softly on the flute. Actually, both muscle conditions – tension and contraction – are present to some degree on every note, regardless of dynamics or range. However, one tends to dominate over the other in accordance with dynamics and range.

Most people instinctively do the wrong thing: they tense up their muscles when playing loud (thus making contraction more difficult), and relax them when playing softly. The result can be poor intonation – the loud notes are played sharp, and soft notes are played flat.

A good exercise is to attack a note softly and then increase it dramatically in volume, or to attack *forte* and diminish to a *pianissimo*. *The purpose of such exercises is to achieve a match between embouchure and breath control.* As you increase the volume of a note, open up your embouchure and contract the muscles of your stomach and sides (but *not* your throat!). As you decrease the volume of a note, close up your embouchure and tense up the muscles of your stomach and sides.

So far we have been talking of changes in the dynamics of a single note. *However, the changes we make in going from loud to soft (or vice versa) on a single note are precisely those we make in changing range on the flute.* In the lower register we play with a large embouchure opening; in the upper register we play with a smaller embouchure opening. Corresponding breath control changes accompany these embouchure changes. For a constant volume of sound, the lower register requires contraction of the muscles of the stomach and sides, and the upper register requires a tension of these muscles.*

This complex interplay of embouchure and breath control muscles is sometimes called "breath support." The expression means that breath control changes must accompany embouchure changes. If they do not, intonation suffers.

Intonation, therefore, is one of the most valuable clues we have as to how well we are matching embouchure and breath control. This is why it is a good idea for a beginning flutist to have access to a well-tuned piano so that he can check on the accuracy with which he is playing notes in all portions of the flute's range. Usually beginners tend to play flat on the low notes and sharp on the high notes. Matching embouchure and breath as we have described above will help to counter this defect.

The "projection" of tone which accomplished musicians can achieve at all dynamic levels throughout the full range of an instrument is the result of carefully matching embouchure and breath control. Either one by itself will not give the desired results. Because students are often more concerned about embouchure than about breath control, we have emphasized the latter to underscore the fact that blowing into the flute is not an aimless or casual act; *it involves the constant, conscientious exercise of the diaphragm and the muscles of the stomach and sides.*

*Changes in range and dynamics can, of course, occur simultaneously. The resulting situation is well described by Philip Farkas, **The Art of Brass Playing** (Brass Publications, Bloomington, Indiana, 1962), pp. 41-42, who says that "a diminuendo during a descending passage will require little or no lip aperture change. An ascending passage requiring a diminuendo will necessitate a drastic lip contraction during the ascent. A descending passage requiring a crescendo will necessitate a drastic enlargement of the aperture during the descent."*

The Throat and Vibrato

About halfway down the neck there is an opening called the glottis (see Figure 50), the size of which is controlled by the "choking" muscle. Like the tongue, the glottis can act as a valve, opening to permit the air column coming up from the lungs to pass freely, or constricting and closing off the air supply.

The glottis is completely closed when we are engaged in an act such as lifting a heavy weight. It is completely open for rapid exhalation, as when we pant like a dog. You can also open your throat to a maximum extent by yawning. When we cough, it is at first tightly closed (while the air pressure below it builds up), and then explodes open so that the resulting rush of air clears our throats.

One of the most common problems for beginning flutists is playing with a tight or constricted throat. This is especially true for the upper octaves of the flute; the higher the student plays, the tighter the throat becomes. As a result, air supply is cut off, the tone thins considerably, and the notes (if a achieved at all) tend to be sharp.

In playing the flute, *the glottis should remain as open as possible at all times,* so that an ample supply of air can be delivered to the embouchure. Many flutists achieve this openness of the throat by pretending that they are just about to yawn before playing a note. *Air supply is then controlled by the breathing muscles of the stomach and sides, not those of the throat.* The one exception to this rule occurs when you use a vibrato, at which time the glottis is opened and partially closed rapidly to modulate the air column.

A good remedy for this situation is to learn conscious control of the choking muscle, i.e., to open and close the glottis at will. Such throat control can be learned through proper vibrato. *Once vibrato has been mastered, the tone is often greatly improved even though the vibrato is not used.* The reason is that in practicing vibrato, the student learns how to control the throat opening, and hence how to deliver an unimpeded air supply to the embouchure. Although vibrato involves both throat and diaphragm muscles, we treat it in this section because of its important bearing on throat control.

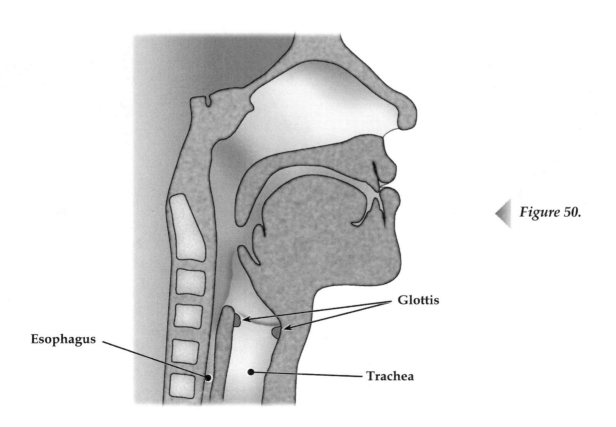

Figure 50.

Glottis

Esophagus

Trachea

The Throat and Vibrato

Vibrato is the name given to the periodic changes in the volume and pitch of a note. Instead of sustaining a tone of constant pitch and volume, the flutist changes the pitch and volume several times per second (usually 4 to 6). As a result the tone seems to pulse or vibrate (hence the name vibrato) and to have more color. It is important to remember that vibrato is surface embellishment or sheen you add to your tone, not a substitute for it.

Vibrato is a controversial subject. Some flutists argue for a vibrato controlled by the diaphragm, and others for a vibrato controlled by the throat. Some argue that vibrato is "natural" and should not be taught. Our position is that vibrato is a useful technique to master, and is best regarded as a modification of the air supply by those muscles which can control it – viz., the diaphragm and related muscles of the abdomen, and the so-called coughing muscle in the throat.

The large diaphragm (and its associated muscles in the abdomen) tends to respond slowly but powerfully, forcing massive pulses of air up through the throat. As a result, a vibrato predominately controlled by the diaphragm is usually slow (3 to 4 beats/second), and wide (i.e., makes large excursions in volume and pitch).

The small muscle in the throat used in coughing or choking can respond so quickly that it has the apparent effect of shutting off and starting the air supply, rather than increasing or decreasing it as does the diaphragm. As a result, a vibrato predominately controlled by the throat tends to be fast and choppy, resulting when greatly exaggerated in a nanny goat-like series of separate notes.

Figure 51.

Figure 52.

Figures 51 & 52. *To experience a closed glottis, take a deep breath, hold it, open your mouth, and try to lift a heavy weight. The air you have inhaled is held in by the closed glottis.*

Figure 53.

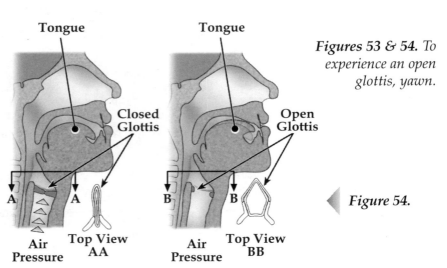

Tongue

Tongue

Closed Glottis

Open Glottis

A   A

B   B

Air Pressure

Top View AA

Air Pressure

Top View BB

Figures 53 & 54. *To experience an open glottis, yawn.*

Figure 54.

When the throat and diaphragm coordinate in vibrato, each helps cancel the undesirable effects of the other. By varying the amount of air supplied to the throat, the pulsations of the diaphragm provide changes in the volume and pitch of the note. The coughing muscle in the throat modulates this varying air supply, gives definition to the individual vibrations, and increases the vibrato rate.

Although throat and diaphragm combine in producing the vibrato, it is a good idea to practice each action separately. For example, keep the diaphragm still and, using a metronome, cough into the flute regularly 3, then 4, then 5 and 6 times per second (m.m. = 60). Gradually elide the series of coughs, smoothing out the separations between them until they blend into one another like a series of waves. Then, hold the throat open and pant into the flute, using the diaphragm to initiate the pulses of air. (You will probably find that you cannot fit more than four such pulses into a one-second interval.)

When you have experienced each of these actions, noted their effect on the tone, and can play them with regularity and evenness, combine the two. Try playing a slow, wide, undulating vibrato (predominantly

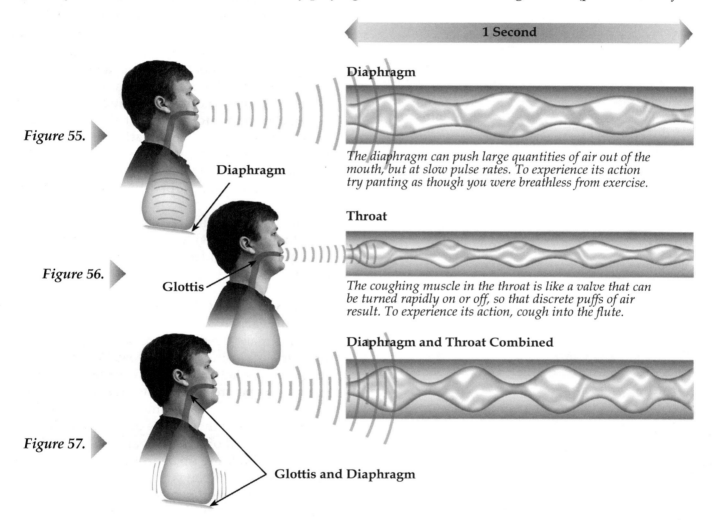

1 Second

Diaphragm

Figure 55.

Diaphragm

The diaphragm can push large quantities of air out of the mouth, but at slow pulse rates. To experience its action try panting as though you were breathless from exercise.

Throat

Figure 56.

Glottis

The coughing muscle in the throat is like a valve that can be turned rapidly on or off, so that discrete puffs of air result. To experience its action, cough into the flute.

Diaphragm and Throat Combined

Figure 57.

Glottis and Diaphragm

diaphragm controlled) whose pulsations you begin to define more sharply by introducing throat control. Try playing a fast vibrato (e.g., six beats per second) with little pitch or volume variation, gradually bringing in the latter two qualities by using the diaphragm. Controlling vibrato *width* is as important as controlling vibrato *speed*. To achieve width control, practice playing sustained notes with a constant vibrato speed and varying the width of the vibrato from wide (large pitch excursions), to medium, to narrow. Then reverse the procedure, starting with a narrow vibrato and gradually increasing its width.

You should be able to play vibratos of varying speeds, widths, and pulse separations, because the musical interpretations you will encounter as a flutist will eventually call for most of the forms of vibrato suggested above for practice.

The Tongue

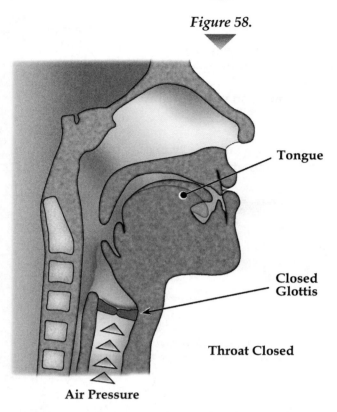

Figure 58.

Tongue

Closed Glottis

Throat Closed

Air Pressure

Figure 58. *Wrong. Do not use the glottis as a valve when tonguing.*

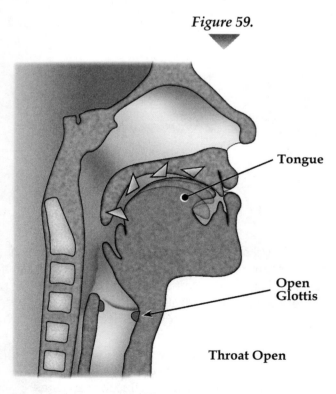

Figure 59.

Tongue

Open Glottis

Throat Open

Figure 59. *Right. Keep throat open and let pressure build up behind the tongue.*

The Tongue

If, prior to playing a note, you have built up sufficient air pressure by contracting and/or tensing the breath control muscles, *the function of the tongue becomes merely that of a valve.* Place your tongue at the top of your mouth, thus closing off the air column, and contract the breath control muscles to build up air pressure. *Tonguing consists of opening up the valves, i.e., getting your tongue out of the way quickly.* This is done by drawing the tongue back, but not to the bottom of the mouth.

Good tonguing (or articulation, as it is sometimes called) *occurs when there is wind pressure behind the tongue prior to tonguing and when that pressure is applied throughout the tongued note.* It is very important to think of your tongue as a releasing device, not a driving or initiating device. If you are controlling the muscles of your sides and stomach correctly, you should have no difficulty in giving a sharp, clear attack to any note. Kincaid used to tell his students that in all articulations, the diaphragm muscles are perhaps as important as the tongue, and warned them to be sure the diaphragm is constantly supporting the articulations.

When you are playing legato (i.e., slurring rather than tonguing notes), your tongue should remain at all times suspended in position for a new attack.

It is important that the tongue, not the glottis, act as the air valve (see Figures 58 and 59). Many students make the mistake of building up air pressure by closing off the throat. When you practice, examine the state of your throat and tongue just before you initiate an attack. Do you feel the air pressure building up directly between your tongue and the surface of your mouth, or have you closed off your throat so that the air pressure is building up beneath your glottis? If the latter is the case, open your throat and let the tongue, not the glottis, serve as the valve. The difference, while subtle, can be felt, and is critical both to good articulation and tone.

While the tongue is used to start notes, it is *not* used to stop them, except when a very abrupt cutoff is called for by the music. Ordinarily, notes are ended by closing (or occasionally opening) the embouchure. This action, as we have pointed out, must be accompanied by an increase in tension (i.e., air pressure) in the muscles of the stomach and sides to prevent the note from going flat.

Our teaching experience leads us to suggest a series of short but concentrated practice sessions (e.g., five to fifteen minutes) each day. Few people can give their full attention to a subject for more than fifteen minutes at a time. Indeed, for most people, the span of concentration is five to ten minutes. Because practicing without concentration is often useless and sometimes harmful, *we recommend a series of short practice periods during which you concentrate solely on a single goal to be accomplished.* You will find these short but concentrated sessions much more fruitful than tedious hours of dutifully "playing exercises."

Too often students regard practicing as a lengthy assigned interval – an hour, for example – which they must spend in aimlessly repeating passages of little musical interest. During this forced session of playing, they daydream about school, sports, or any number of subjects while making sound on a musical instrument. The result is often a frustrating waste of time which improves neither technique nor temper. Indeed, such "practice sessions" often degrade rather than improve performance. Further, since improvement comes slowly if at all, students increasingly begrudge the large amounts of time they spend "practicing" without apparent purpose or results. Many times problems in learning to play a musical instrument stem from this intellectual failure – i.e., an inability to concentrate on a subject for any length of time – rather than from lack of talent or application.

In the preceding paragraphs we have implied a distinction between practicing (concentrating on a single thing to be accomplished) and "playing exercises." There are many other differences between the two. In practicing we often have to make unmusical sounds. For example, if you are learning to attack notes properly and are concentrating on tongue placement and air pressure, you may find that the note you happen to be fingering cracks upward to a false (harmonic) note. This is perfectly all right. *The good student will accept the faulty sounds* and continue to concentrate on air pressure and tongue. Only when these things have been practiced for a while will the student adjust his or her lips so that the note no longer cracks. Poor or mediocre students, on the other hand, often insist that their playing sound "pretty" at all times, and hence make it difficult for themselves to learn.

The art of practicing is well described with respect to tennis by W.W. Sawyer, who says that "you should not begin by trying to strike the ball into the court, but…by hitting it hard, and with good style. Gradually you will find that the ball begins to land in the court. If you start by worrying about where the ball goes, you will always be a feeble player."*

*W.W. Sawyer, **Mathematician's Delight** (Penguin Books, Baltimore, Maryland, 1954, p. 24.

A Word About Practice

Learning to play the flute develops control over many parts of your body such as the lips, fingers, and breathing apparatus. Some of these can only be trained by practicing on the flute. Others, however, can be helped substantially by doing things that have no apparent relationship to the flute yet are often useful forms of practice. For example, sit-up exercises are excellent for developing those muscles of the sides and stomach which play such an important role in keeping up a constant-pressure air stream. The late William Kincaid attributed his extraordinary breath control to extensive practice as a swimmer, and recommended long-distance running as a means of improving diaphragmatic breathing. In this book we have suggested forms of exercise which do not involve the flute yet have a direct bearing upon your ability to play it. Such exercises are as important as those written out in musical form and should be considered a form of practice. They are merely more direct (and hence less time consuming) ways of dealing with the muscles and tendons of your body.

By practicing we mean doing something right repeatedly. Therefore, we suggest that whatever you practice, you *practice very slowly and correctly. If you play things fast and incorrectly, you are practicing errors,* and regressing rather than progressing. This is a simple and obvious rule, yet people so often forget it when practicing that it is a good idea to write it prominently as a motto on the wall of your practice room.

Finally, *practicing is a time for experimentation.* Do not be afraid to try unusual lip placements and formations to see what happens to your tone. Try changing radically the angle at which you blow, the amount of tension in your lips, the size of the opening between your teeth, etc. Learn what effects such changes have on the kind of sound you produce and the amount of control you can exert. Learning anything involves constant experimentation, adjustment, and understanding. Often in trying out what appear to us to be extremes, we discover very useful techniques. In any case, *finding what not to do is sometimes as important as finding what to do.*

Summary

To help you keep in mind the main points of our discussion as you practice, we list them here in tabular form. We suggest that you review them before each practice session as a kind of check list of things to keep in mind.

1   Practice things slowly, correctly, and with full concentration on the single thing you are trying to learn.

2   The flute is balanced, not held; keep your fingers as free as possible

3   Proper posture is essential to good breathing, good tone, and accurate fingering.

4   Inhale by depressing the diaphragm. Exhale by pulling on the muscles of the stomach and sides. Control by keeping the abdominal muscles firm during exhalation.

5   Watch your embouchure in a mirror to make sure that the opening between your lips is a gentle ellipse ⬭, not a stretched ellipse ⬭.

6   Your embouchure should be firm, but not taut.

7   To find the right embouchure for a note, experiment by changing the size of the lip opening, the orifice-to-edge distance, and the angle at which you are blowing.

8   Match embouchure and air supply by drawing in and/or tensing the muscles of the stomach and sides.

9   Think of your tongue as a valve whose chief function is to get out of the way of a pressurized column of air.

10   Control the expenditure of the air supply with the muscles of the stomach and sides, not those of the throat. Keep mouth and throat as open as possible.

Exercises

Balancing (see page 4 and following)

1. Slowly

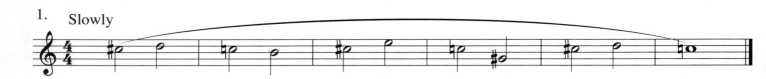

Breathing (see page 11 and following)

2.

Play the above exercise as softly as possible
A. Metronome setting in the beginning - 60
B. Time the duration of each day and increase length of time in one breath (use increasingly slower metronome setting)

Embouchure (see page 18 and following)

3.

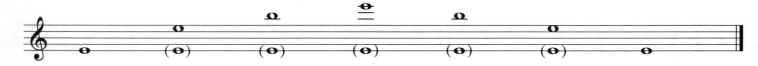

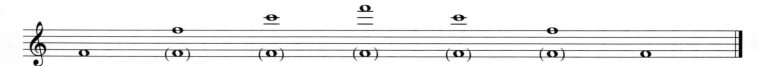

Practice the above exercise by:
A. Fingering the lowest note (fundamental)
B. Playing the other notes (harmonics) by changing the embouchure

Do Not increase volume for higher notes

Dynamics (see page 25 and following)

4.

Dynamics and Embouchure Exercise (see page 25 and following)

5.

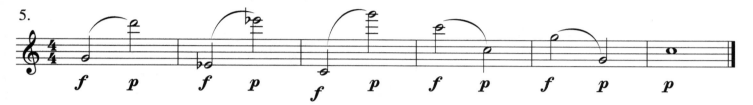

Vibrato (see page 27 and following)

6.

Practice similar sustained notes in all registers:
A. Metronome setting = 60
B. Practice 2 per beat, 3 per beat, 4 per beat, 5 per beat
C. Practice
    1. Diaphragm vibrato
    2. Throat vibrato
    3. Vibrato using both diaphragm and throat

Intonation (see page 25 and following)

7.

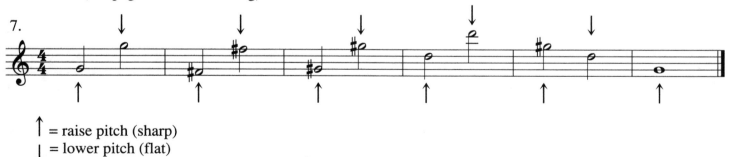

↑ = raise pitch (sharp)
↓ = lower pitch (flat)

Finger coordination (see page 4 through 8)

8.

*(1st finger)

Practice the above as shown, one octave higher, staccato and slurred

*Slurring (see page 20)

9.

10.

*Flute is not rolled during register changes

Balancing the flute (see page 4 and following)

11.

*keep LH 1st finger raised on D♮

Practice the above as shown, one octave higher, staccato and slurred

12.

** keep LH 1st finger raised on D♯

Practice the above as shown, one octave higher, staccato and slurred

Two chromatic scales

13.

scale written in sharps

14.

scale written in flats

Suggestions for Practicing the Daily Exercises

Suggestions for Practicing the Daily Exercises

The exercises which follow have been carefully designed to meet the general requirements of the flute for almost any musical situation. Playing the flute can be reduced essentially to making controlled changes from one note to another with different dynamics, articulations, attacks, and tonal variations. The exercises were constructed by first analyzing and enumerating all the intervals possible within the compass of the instrument, then devising exercises so that each interval occurs at least once. The Solos have been designed to expose the student to problems of contemporary music. Not only do they contain unusual scales and tonal series, but the pieces also make use of special effects such as triple tones, quarter-tones, little-used attacks, and key vibratos. Students who need more information on performing contemporary techniques should see the more detailed book and CD *Special Effects For Flute* by **Sheridon Stokes and Richard Condon (Trio Associates, 1970).**

Hints for performing the exercises

Tempo: Play at a very comfortable speed so that the interval changes are controlled and accurate.

Dynamics: Play each exercise piano, mezzoforte, forte, or with crescendos in ascending and descending passages.

Rhythms: Vary the articulations and rhythmic patterns. For example, use each of these articulations:

Registers: When possible, play exercises an octave higher.

Note: *Play the exercises slowly, without stopping, or going back to correct mistakes.* To correct mistakes practice the passage (including the notes before and after) several times after completing the entire exercise.

5. *Note scales using all possible combinations of major and minor thirds (also play 8va, staccato and legato)

15.

6. Note scales (also play 8va, staccato and legato)

16.

*Note scales - non traditional scale patterns

8. Note scales (diminished scales) with alternating half-steps and whole-steps (also play 8va staccato and legato)

17.

Arpeggios of alternating major-minor thirds (also play staccato and legato)

18.

Arpeggios of increasing intervals (also play staccato and legato)

19.

Arpeggios of decreasing intervals (also play staccato and legato)

20.

Broken arpeggios of increasing intervals (also play 8va, staccato and legato)

21.

Broken arpeggios of decreasing intervals (also play staccato and legato)

22.

Arpeggios consisting of all major thirds and all minor thirds (also play 8va, staccato and legato)

23.

Fourths and tritones (also play staccato and legato)

24.

A twelve-tone row and its retrograde inversion (practice the following forwards and backwards - all tempos)

25.

*retrograde inversion starts here

Two variations

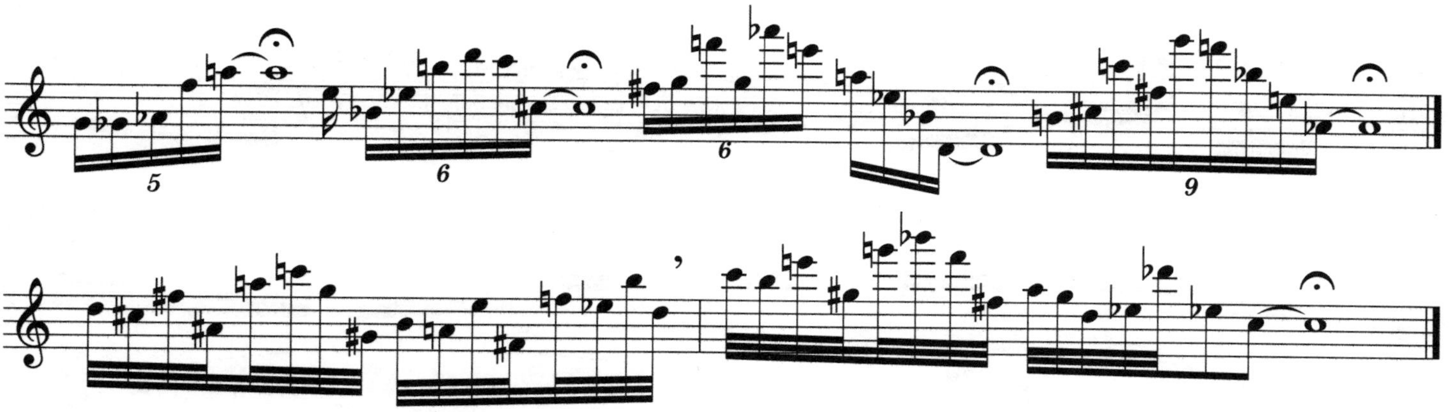

5

6

6

9

43

Etude-1

John Neufeld

44

45

Etude-2

John Neufeld

Light and staccato (♩ = 120-140)

47

Etude-3

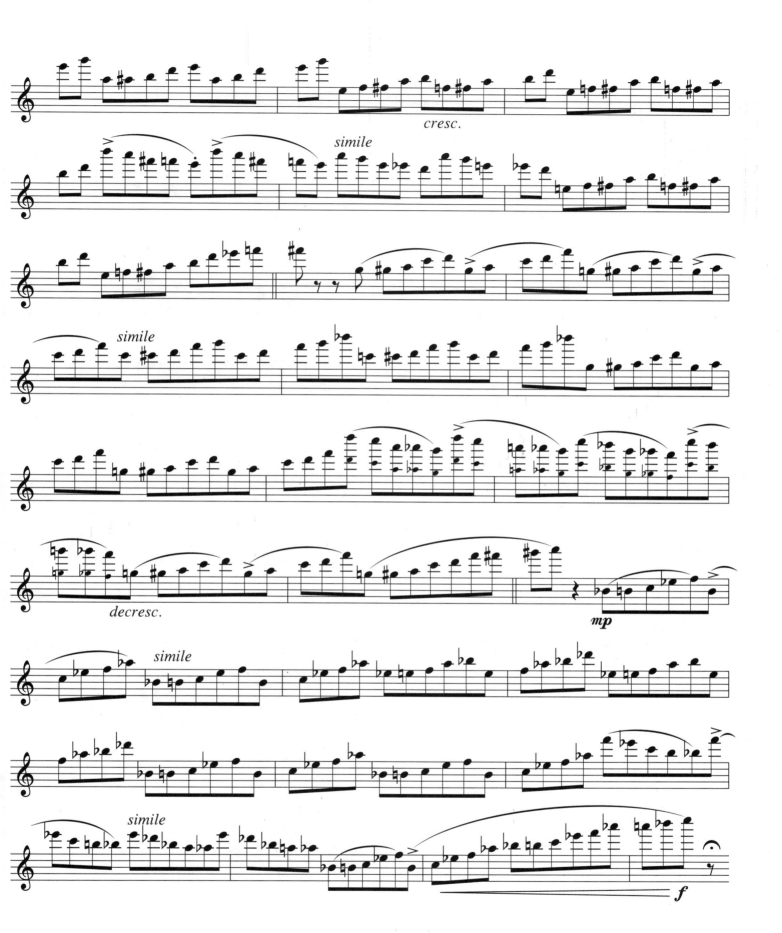

49

Etude-4

♩ = 96-133 (play with Metronome)

John Neufeld

52

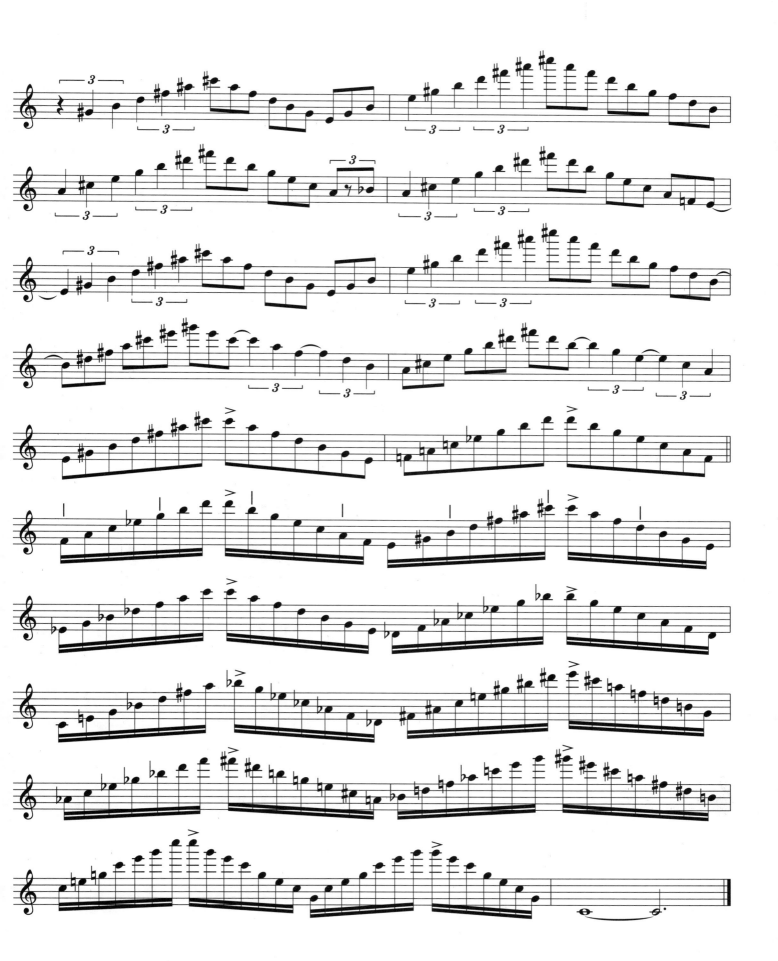

53

Etude-5

John Neufeld

(open embouchure)

56

Ikhofi Dance*

Solo Bass Flute and Alto Flute

♩ = 70 Very free tempo *(a piacere)*

Sheridon Stokes (1993)

Bass Flute *(C Flute)*

*Recording available on Wild New Music for Flute CD by Sheridon Stokes and Jared Ferguson

58

59

The Illustrated Method Fingering Chart

This chart gives fingerings for both the standard C flute and the alternate model with a low B foot joint. The three and one half octaves illustrated cover the entire range of the flute. To use the chart, find the note you want to play and press down the keys indicated in grey. The number of the finger used is shown on the key. Fingerings are numbered for quick reference by the teacher or the student. Alternate fingerings (sometimes useful for rapid execution or good intonation) are also included in the chart.

1st Octave

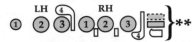

① B

② C

③ C#{D♭}

** Press Two Keys With One Finger

④ D

⑤ D#{E♭}

⑥ E

⑦ F

⑧ F#{G♭}

Alternate Fingering

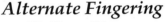

⑨ F#{G♭}

⑩ G

⑪ G#{A♭}

⑫ A

㉘ A#{B♭}

Alternate Fingering

⑭ A#{B♭}

⑮ B

 60

2nd Octave

⑯ C

⑰ C#{D♭}

⑱ D

⑲ D#{E♭}

⑳ E

㉑ F

㉒ F#{G♭}

Alternate Fingering

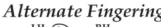

㉓ F#{G♭}

㉔ G

㉕ G#{A♭}

㉖ A

㉗ A#{B♭}

Alternate Fingering

㉘ A#{B♭}

㉙ B

61

3rd Octave

(30) C

(31) C#{D♭}

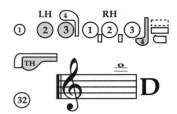
(32) D

(33) D#{E♭}

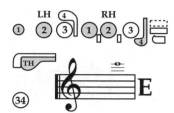
(34) E

(35) F

(36) F#{G♭}

Alternate Fingering

(37) F#{G♭}

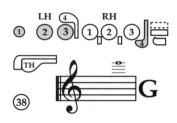
(38) G

(39) G#{A♭}

Alternate Fingering

(40) G#{A♭}

(41) A

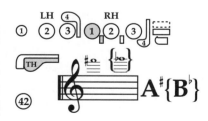
(42) A#{B♭}

Alternate Fingering

(43) A#{B♭}

(44) B

4th Octave

㊺ **C**

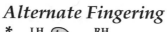

* ㊻ **C**

* For Flute With Low B

㊼ **C#{Db}**

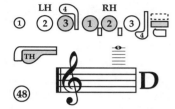

㊽ **D**

* ㊾ **D#{Eb}**

* For Flute With Low B

* ㊿ **D#{Eb}**

* For Flute With Low C
** Press Two Keys With One Finger

(51) **E**

(52) **F**

63

Books and CDs Available From Sheridon Stokes Music

Suite for Flute & Piano, Explorations: 1980
by Bill Mays

Recorded by Bud Shank and Bill Mays for Concord Concerto-CC2002. This innovative five movement suite draws from both classical and jazz forms and calls for flute as well as piano, improvising in all but one of the movements.

Special Effects for Flute
by Sheridon Stokes and Richard Condon

Covers all the special effects necessary for the performance of contemporary music, including jazz. Quarter tones, sub-tones, double- and triple-tones, etc.

Includes demo CD (also available separately).

Six Jazz Flute Duets
by Lennie Niehaus

Lennie Niehaus is a household word among jazz musicians. Having been a phenomenal jazz saxophonist, he is eminently qualified to write for and understand woodwind instruments. These duets fill a need for jazz flute literature, since in the past most duets were written for saxophone or clarinet. The six duets in this book will be a valuable addition to any flutist's repertoire.

Wild New Music for Flute
Sheridon Stokes and Jared Ferguson

All original music that employs the extremely broad range of tonal colors the flute is capable of producing.

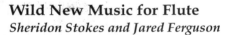

Ardiente
Christopher Caliendo with Sheridon Stokes

Sheridon Stokes and Christopher Caliendo combine their talents again on this second collection of American Tangos. A fiery outpouring of Latin passion and soulful artistry.

Torbellino
Christopher Caliendo with Sheridon Stokes

A collection of 10 original American Tangos performed by Christopher Caliendo, composer/guitarist and the legendary flutist Sheridon Stokes. Featuring *La Milonga*, the NFA Winner for Newly Published Flute Music 2000.

Also available - The Illustrated Method for Flute companion CD, with narrated text, musical scores and accompanying exercises.

Please visit our website for current pricing information: **www.flute-music.com**

To place an order please contact Sheridon Stokes Music at: **(310) 477-7048**, or via email: **ssmpublish@aol.com**

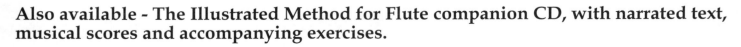

Notes

Notes

Notes